I Love Horses!

By Tagore Ramoutar

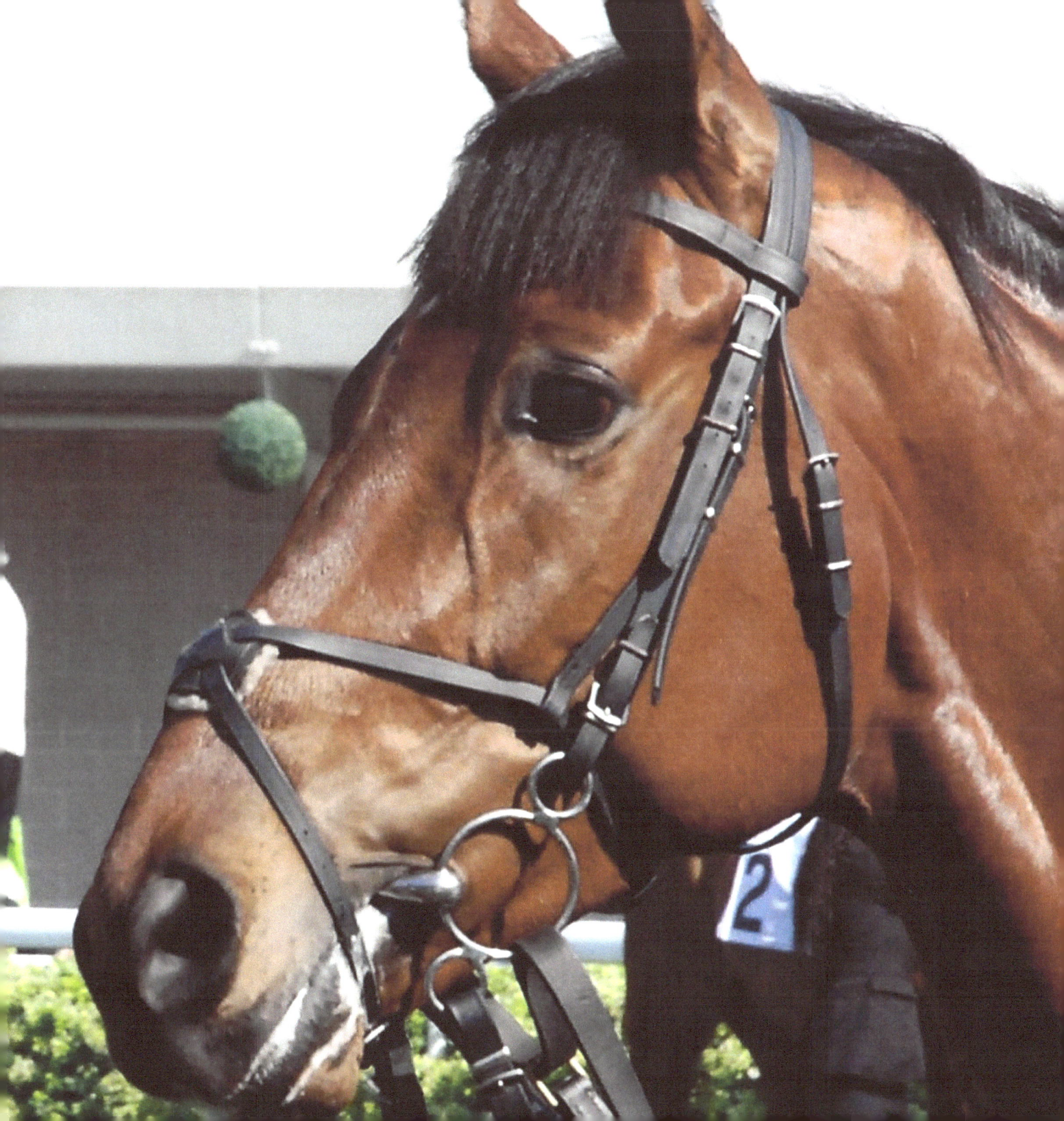

First Published 2015.
Published by under name Eric and Rufus Children's Books, a brand of Longshot Ventures Ltd, UK. Copyright Tagore Ramoutar, Longshot Ventures Ltd.
Printed in the UK / USA.

Lightning Source ISBN 978-1-907837-84-5.
Amazon ISBN 978-1-907837-85-2.

The rights of Tagore Ramoutar to be identified as the author and illustrator of this work has been asserted by him in accordance with the Copyright, Designs and Patents Act, 1988.

www.ericandrufus.com

www.ingramcontent.com/pod-product-compliance
Lightning Source LLC
Chambersburg PA
CBHW040025050426
42452CB00003B/134